Praise

"When you live a restless, writerly life, as Lang does, moving here, immigrating there (America, France, Israel), you need to discover, or invent, a literary structure as sophisticated and beautifully complicated as the life it replicates. Which she does. Each facet in this collection is its own world-in-miniature that ultimately coheres into a compelling whole."

SUE WILLIAM SILVERMAN, AUTHOR OF
HOW TO SURVIVE DEATH AND OTHER INCONVENIENCES

"Love is unpredictable, as is language and the forms our stories take on the page. In her memoir-in-miniature, *Places We Left Behind*, Jennifer Lang offers readers a compelling tale of unexpected commitment alongside unconventional nonfiction exploration."

DINTY W. MOORE, AUTHOR OF *BETWEEN PANIC & DESIRE*

"Jennifer Lang's *Places We Left Behind* reminds us in arresting lyrical essays that life and love are always fraught, always tentative, always complex. Add to the mix an international marriage, different levels of religious observance, and raising children in both the USA and Israel amidst ongoing conflict, and we have the recipe for gripping, surprising reading. I read eagerly awaiting where we'd land next and what form the visit would take."

PATRICK MADDEN, AUTHOR OF *DISPARATES*

"Humor and being real gets me every time. Thank you Jennifer for hitting the funny bone with so much wisdom on love."

RODNEY YEE, INTERNATIONAL YOGA TEACHER, AUTHOR, AND
CO-CREATOR OF URBAN ZEN INTEGRATIVE THERAPY

"Jennifer Lang's *Places We Left Behind* is an utterly engaging journey. It's a poetic, playful and sometimes painful story of marriage, perseverance, commitment, and most of all love—for our families, our partners and finally—ourselves."

CORIE ADJMI, AWARD-WINNING AUTHOR OF
LIFE AND OTHER SHORTCOMINGS

"How refreshing: A memoir pared down to its barest essentials, in spare, lucid prose. In *Places We Left Behind*, Jennifer Lang crafts the story of her marriage into a fascinating exploration of how to juxtapose one's own happiness with the sacrifices needed to please the other."

EVAN FALLENBERG, AUTHOR OF *THE PARTING GIFT*

"In this highly engaging and highly hybrid memoir, Jennifer Lang has created a smart and compelling narrative about the twists and turns of a relationship when religion, identity, and a sense of place are focal points. With inventive structures that enhance the narrative's tone and action, this mesmerizing love story is irresistible."

CHELSEY CLAMMER, AUTHOR OF *HUMAN HEARTBEAT DETECTED*

"*Places We Left Behind* is a powerful memoir that delves into the complexities of love, loss, and self-discovery. Lang examines the intricacies of marriage and compromise with poetic grace and raw honesty. For anyone who has ever loved deeply and been willing to take risks for the sake of love."

RACHEL BARENBAUM AUTHOR OF *ATOMIC ANNA*

"Jennifer shares her strengths and vulnerabilities. Her unique journey is inspiring and thought provoking. While the journey is unique, the story is relatable and reminds us all that our life practice requires courage and self-compassion."

SUSAN RUBIN, OWNER OF SUSAN RUBIN WELLNESS

About the Author

Born in the San Francisco Bay Area, Jennifer Lang lives in Tel Aviv, where she runs Israel Writers Studio. Her essays have appeared in *Baltimore Review, Crab Orchard Review, Under the Sun, Ascent, Consequence*, and elsewhere. A Pushcart Prize and Best American Essays nominee, she holds an MFA from Vermont College of Fine Arts and serves as an assistant editor for *Brevity: A Journal of Concise Literary Nonfiction*. Often findable on her yoga mat—practicing since 1995, teaching since 2003—with her legs up her living room wall. *Places We Left Behind* is her first book and *Landed: A yogi's memoir in pieces & poses* will follow in October 2024.

israelwriterstudio.com

PLACES
We Left
BEHIND

a memoir-in-miniature

Jennifer Lang

www.vineleavespress.com

Print Edition
ISBN: 978-3-98832-018-6
Published by Vine Leaves Press 2023

Cover design by Jessica Bell
Interior design by Amie McCracken

Mom and Dad, thank you for letting me fly far
and for always welcoming me home.

To my three (young adult) munchkins,
may you also fly far and know אֶבָּא and I are here,
home, thrilled to see you.

A mon prince, je t' ♡
beaucoup *beaucoup* **beaucoup!**

Contents

Author's Note

The vignettes in this book reflect my recollection of events, my emotional truth. I did not change anyone's name but did not name certain family members or fully flesh them out as secondary characters to respect their wishes. I refer to my one sibling as Sib for the sake of privacy. I also took select creative liberties, recreating dialogue as accurately as memory allows for the sake of the narrative.

For my first 18 years

I sleep in the same room (opposite my parents) in the same house (116 Monticello Avenue) in the same city (Piedmont) in the same state (CA) in the same country (USA), but soon after leaving for college in Evanston, IL, I pine for elsewhere and end up peripatetic...

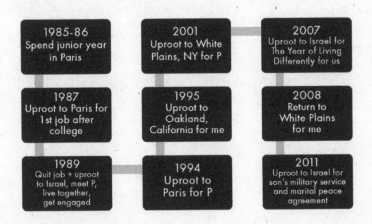

1985-86 Spend junior year in Paris

2001 Uproot to White Plains, NY for P

2007 Uproot to Israel for The Year of Living Differently for us

1987 Uproot to Paris for 1st job after college

1995 Uproot to Oakland, California for me

2008 Return to White Plains for me

1989 Quit job + uproot to Israel, meet P, live together, get engaged

1994 Uproot to Paris for P

2011 Uproot to Israel for son's military service and marital peace agreement

Conjunctions

After making love on his mismatched sheets, Philippe and I tally how many times we've each been to Israel. I count my trips—1971, 1975, 1981, 1983, 1984, 1985, 1988, now in 1989—needing both hands.

He counts his on one hand: ‖‖. *You win,* he says, as if we're competing.

I scan his room—no posters, no mirror, no night-stand—so boyish and beautiful, especially his bed.

Tell me everything, he says, adorning me with butterfly light kisses.

My tendency to share too much too soon makes me hesitate. He already knows that I'm here despite the First Intifada or Palestinian uprising, between a job in France and graduate school in New York, to immerse in Hebrew as well as to spend time with my only sibling and extended family, and that I miss my open-minded, California-born parents in the San Francisco Bay Area, but he has no idea that I made a Jackson Pollock mess of my love life the past two years and promised my mother that I wouldn't fall in love and stay.

No, wait, I want to know why you're here, I say, running my fingers through his silky chestnut hair. *What made you immigrate?*

Israeli chutzpah, Haifa, the Mediterranean, beach, bodysurfing, falafel, spicy food. Plus, my brother plans to make aliya too.

We each have one sibling; mine immigrated to Jerusalem, my temporary home base, immediately after college a few years earlier.

And since aliya comes from the verb la'a lot, which means to go up, I went up in my Jewish observance. Tu comprends?

Do I understand that he changed his lifestyle for a country? ~~Absolutely not.~~

All weekend, I study this man, admiring how his pointy nose dominates an angular face, his olive skin glistens with oily patches, and his feet have white lines underneath his sandal straps.

All weekend, he reaches for me, amorous and solicitous of my attention.

Ever since we met at a *Shabbat* retreat for Francophones 144 hours earlier, I haven't stopped thinking about him, convinced my secular mother will tell me it was *beshert*—Yiddish for destiny—after enrolling me in a pilot French program when I was six.

Philippe fits every box on my imaginary list:

French

Jewish

Smart ✓

Single ✓

Sexy with a guarded smile ✓

A far cry from the men of late: one Catholic Parisian whom Sib refused to acknowledge, one Russian married man who my parents refused to discuss, one once-upon-a-time college friend who refused to commit.

Burrowed in Philippe's biceps, I try to block out the conjunctions: *if* he wasn't Sabbath observant, *and* he wasn't enrapt with his new homeland, *but* he is.

Between seams

    The following weekend,
I show Philippe my favorite Jerusalem haunts
in the Old City.

    Hands clasped,
we enter through Jaffa Gate and

                        zig-
    zag

        through the Arab souk
                in the Muslim Quarter,
                down the alleys
        toward the Cardo, the city's main street
1500 years ago,

                        in the Jewish one.
    The scent of sesame pretzels mixed with
fried falafel mixed with cat piss taunts me.

                        At the top of the stairs,
~~before the security checkpoint facing the Temple~~
~~Mount,~~ above the

        Wailing   Wall,
                we   stop.

How many times have I stood in this spot?

        Yet,   every   time   feels   different,
hypnotic,   like
stepping into the pages of a 10th-grade World History
textbook.

      A powerful force, a physical and emotional
      sense of belonging, makes me sigh.

                              Gazing
at the ancient limestone wall,
      the gold Dome of the Rock,
           a Muslim minaret,
  and the olive trees   beyond,
                          I pause.

At the bottom of the stairs, we part ways to enter
the men's and women's sections, where countless
white slips of paper—notes and prayers, wishes and
dreams—nestle in its cracks, between its seams.

My wish list is simple:
              no more violence,
     no more war,
          no more Israel Defense Forces.*

  NO MORE! NO MORE! NO MORE! NO
YOU-KNOW-WHO DAMN MORE! ENOUGH!

Minutes later, I spot Philippe walking away from
the Wall backwards and beam.

                  *Add to wish list: more of this man

Room

Can you wait outside? Philippe asks on Friday morning.

Sure. (What the hell is his problem?) I open and close his bedroom door. (Listen or walk away?) I head to the kitchen for a cup of Nescafé. (Do I want to date someone with secrets?)

He finds me on the living room sofa. Before I can ask what or why, he says *when I was thirteen, my father taught me how to put on tefillin for my bar mitzvah.* I know they're the set of small black leather boxes containing scrolls of parchment inscribed with verses from the Torah that men put on their forehead and finger but have never seen anyone wrap them. *I've been doing it every day since then.*

Okay, I say. (Am I okay?) (Just how Jewish is this man?) (Do I want to be with someone so Jewish?)

I wasn't sure what you'd think. Because of Sib. You know?

Only together three weekends, he already knows a lot about me and my hang-ups.

In the small residential city of Piedmont, with less than 0.5% Jews, my parents picked and chose when

19

to be Jewish. On Rosh Hashanah and Yom Kippur, my father forced us to go to temple. On Passover, we dumped Ding Dongs and Ho Hos in the basement freezer, stacked Manischewitz macaroons and gefilte fish in kitchen cupboards, and brought PB&J sandwiches on matzo to school. On Friday nights, I went to school dances; on Saturdays, we yanked weeds in our backyard before U.C. Berkeley football games. But my identity was strong, cemented by five summers at Camp Swig and leadership positions in National Federation of Temple Youth. Since immigrating to Israel, Sib veered from our family, chose a different path, based on the Torah and laws, landing on the far-right side of the spectrum. ~~Think Kosher Kool-Aid.~~

Where does Philippe's traditional upbringing with kosher kitchen, synagogue on *Shabbat* and meals at home (Friday night dinner and Saturday lunch) then bike riding and mischief making with friends, plus public school, Hebrew school, and Jewish summer camp, fall?

Lying prone on his scratchy sofa, I motion for him to come closer, longing to feel his body brush against mine. Where he falls is still unclear, but I'm falling for, falling fast, falling deeply.

Sides

After four weekends of commuting, Philippe proposes we live together *chez lui*. My cheeks puff with disbelief. If we tally up our time together, it's been a mere eleven days, 264 hours, 15,840 minutes, or 950,400 seconds.

After I replay his proposal for Andrea, my old camp friend here for the first year of Reform rabbinic school, suggests I make a pro-con list.

I love the neatness of two columns: words, phrases, or sentences battling it out on opposite sides of a piece of paper. I draw a vertical line down the middle of a page in my right-to-left Hebrew notebook and write:

+	-
- learn everything about Philippe & Hebrew	- impending departure for grad school
- see great aunt/uncle/ cuz's in Hadera more often	-no meaningful job/ career path

- spend time with old friends, make new ones	- no backup plan if we break-up
	- too far from home
	- protests & riots
	- religious differences/ incompatibility

When the negatives outweigh the positives,
I tear out the sheet and toss it.

Seesaw

After another four weekends of back-and-forth bus rides, I pack my worldly belongings into two duffel bags and unpack into Philippe's floor-to-ceiling cupboards. One sweltering Friday afternoon, I find him brooding in our bedroom and ask what's wrong.

Do you think you could do Shabbat more like me?

Every seven days, we dance around it. If we spend the twenty-five hours[1] with my non-observant friends, we discuss in advance if he'll eat a vegetarian meal in a non-kosher kitchen, if he'll tolerate a television blaring or lights turning on and off. Conversely, if we spend it with religious friends, if I'll agree to sleep separately or dress modestly as if on opposing ends of a teeter totter:

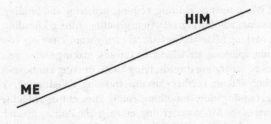

---

[1] As if twenty-four isn't enough, the extra hour is to *add from the profane to the holy*

Where he feels comfortable, I'm ill-at-ease.

Unlike my *baal-teshuva* or returnee-to-religion Sib, who tears toilet paper and switches off the refrigerator light before ushering in the Sabbath (two of too many technicalities), Philippe isn't a stickler for the minutiae underlying the 39^2 prohibitions. He enjoys the big picture: no driving, no using electricity, no spending money. But if I don't believe in god, why would I believe in his commandment to keep the day of rest? Why would I stop doing any of the seemingly mundane activities I don't consider prohibited?

But if neither one of us is willing to yield, where will that leave us?

Fine, I capitulate. *I'll try my best to respect your rules, but I'll always eat in anyone's house and every restaurant.*

Philippe shrugs.

Some phantom weight slides from his shoulders onto mine.

---

[2] Field Work: sowing, plowing, reaping, gathering and binding, threshing, winnowing, selecting, grinding, sifting, kneading, baking; Making Material Curtains: shearing wool, cleaning, combing, dyeing, spinning, stretching the threads, making loops, weaving threads, separating threads, tying knots, untying knots, sewing, tearing; Making Leather Curtains: trapping, slaughtering, skinning, tanning hide, smoothing, ruling lines, cutting; Making the Beams of the Mishkan: writing, erasing; The Putting up and Taking down of the Mishkan: building, demolishing; The Mishkan's Final Touches: extinguishing fire, kindling fire, striking final hammer blow, carrying

Never ever

When I awaken to an empty bed, I follow my nose. Odors of breakfast drift down the hall, toward the galley kitchen. As batter hits butter, hissing sounds sing.

Joyeux anniversaire, he says.

In a fitted t-shirt and floral boxers, Philippe flips crepes single handedly. A sight I've never seen before. No man has ever made me crepes; no Frenchman has ever made me crepes; no any-nationality man has ever made me crepes.

Summer heat and sexual desire swarm my every cell. He tells me to sit, serves me impeccably round, thin, buttery crepes. I watch his string-bean-long legs cavort in the confined space, hearing my brain croon words like stay, forever, keep him while striving to ignore the others about distance, religion, and political climate. It's not a perfect fit, and I'm old enough to know better.

Him, me, us

As soon as the High Holiday season ends, the country reopens at green-light speed. While I memorize Hebrew verbs in *ulpan* and edit academic papers, in English, for Haifa University professors, Philippe searches for chemical engineering jobs. In early December, Israel Electric Corporation offers him a full-time position. His future is set.

Bundled in sweatshirts and turtlenecks to keep warm in the poorly insulated apartment, we dine at the wobbly kitchen table. He slurps spaghetti, splattering rosé sauce. I weigh an M.A. in international relations here with no clear profession versus an M.A. in public policy there with the goal to make learning foreign languages mandatory in elementary school. He stops mid-slurp.

It's your decision, he says, gliding my chair toward his.

For months, I've toyed with staying. Wondered if it satisfies some yearning to see if I belong, like Sib, like Philippe. Or, is the decision to stay so entangled in our relationship that I cannot separate what I want from where I want to be?

I'd love it. But it has to be for you, he says.

Every pronoun I've ever learned—in English, French, Hebrew—from him and me, to *lui et moi,* to הוא ואני blurs.

Pang

One Friday morning, we ride a bus to Hadar, a working-class neighborhood halfway down Carmel Mountain, to *Shabbat* shop at the souk.

Everybody says Haifa resembles San Francisco, Philippe says.

He's never been to the City by the Bay (or to the United States for that matter), but I've heard many Israelis liken the two. Both share steep, windy streets and water, but all similarities end there.

Out the bus window, I glimpse a neglected port, power plant, oil refinery, and random towers next to dilapidated buildings under puffs of pollution. Incomparable vis-à-vis the fog-enveloped vermillion Golden Gate Bridge, cable cars at Little-Engine-That-Could pace, or Coit Tower aglow from miles away. A pang of homesickness stings like a hornet.

Naïve

Eight months after our first kiss, seconds after opening our eyes one Sunday morning, our phone rings. My mother tells me she needs braces and doesn't want them on for pictures, so can we please give her a date for the wedding? Thanks to her boundary-breaking chutzpah, we decide on the following September.

Since the only way to marry legally in Israel is with the Chief Rabbinate, the authoritative body controlling Jewish marriage and divorce, we hire an American-born Orthodox rabbi in khaki pants, polo t-shirt, and penny loafers, who instantly understands our differing levels of observance and asks how religious we want the ceremony.

When I suggest we tweak a biblical tradition whereby the bride circles the groom seven times to show how she figuratively builds the walls of the couple's new world together and each circle one another half, Philippe agrees. When I propose my female cousin holds one of the *chuppah* poles, an honor customarily reserved for men, nobody objects.

But, the rabbi reminds me, I have to go to the *mikve*. I know but begrudge a bunch of bureaucratic, god-fearing strangers requiring me to dunk in the ritual bath, naked, for some woman to inspect and bless me in order for our union to be recognized by the State of Israel.

After our meeting, I relax, confident the hard part is behind us. I'm so, so naïve.

Stuck

Weeks before our nuptials,

1019 miles east,

Saddam Hussein invades

Kuwait and threatens to

attack Israel, and I want to

scream

—at the nonstop news

headlines, the irrational Iraqi

president,

my foolhardy decision to

abandon my plans and stay in

this unstable region—

but sound sticks to the sides

of my throat like dried glue.

How?

On the second Sunday in September (and a super cool, difficult-to-forget date: 9-9-90), Philippe and I occupy separate parts of Mei Niftowach, a restaurant overlooking Jerusalem's valleys to the north. While he listens to the rabbi read the *ketubah,* detailing the rights and responsibilities of the groom toward the bride, I pose for pictures on the outdoor terrace like Lady Di. We haven't seen each other since Friday in an attempt to uphold part of the customary week-long separation between a bride and groom. My insides burn with desire.

At nightfall on that halcyon evening, we stand under the fire-orange embroidered *chuppah,* under the stars, surrounded by 100 guests. Philippe lowers my veil, a safeguard made by Jewish males since Jacob wed a veiled Leah in error. Our bicultural, bilingual rabbi asks us if we promise to love, cherish and protect each other, whether in good fortune or in adversity, and to seek with each other a life hallowed by the faith of Israel. I say yes without thinking about the words.

As I slip a ring on Philippe's finger, I think about how he blinks his eyes like an impish little boy, how he looks like he does dozens of push-ups every day, how he makes jokes with a straight face. How we are going to spend our lives together. ~~How are we going to spend our lives together?~~

Jitters

Do you feel like we just made things complicated?
Philippe asks.

We'd less than twenty-four hours earlier and en route to France, I lean my head against his shoulder for take-off. My body fits seamlessly against his whether sitting, standing, or supine.

My parents are in one country, yours in another, and we're in a third, he says.

Our new reality sounds daunting; to see our folks, we have to spend a lot of money, use vacation time, and traverse several time zones.

How about we spend seven years in Israel, seven in France, and seven in America? Deal? I suggest, convinced it's the ideal solution.

In Judaism, seven's super symbolic: the number of *aliyot*[3] on *Shabbat*, the number of times a Torah is carried around the synagogue on Simchat Torah[4],

---

[3] the act of being called to and reading a portion from the Torah
[4] the holiday marking the end of the annual cycle of public Torah readings and the beginning of a new one

and the number of times *when a man takes a wife* appears in the Bible[5].

Philippe laughs, *If you want.*

Midair, I stare out the window at Tel Aviv's hodge-podge of skyscrapers and patches of green, at the ancient port city of Jaffa and its red-and-white lighthouse. As we climb in altitude, I'm hovering, unmoored.

---

[5] totally paltry compared to how many times mine has taken me

In denial

Back in Haifa, we unpack wedding presents. Boxes litter the living room carpet. I prop crystal vases in a glass cabinet and stack ceramic serving dishes in the sideboard. Overnight, our newlywed apartment looks grown-up and serious.

I lift matching bulky boxes—His-and-Hers gas masks, unwanted and unwelcome gifts from the Israeli government—with hunched shoulders and a clueless expression.

Follow me, Philippe says.

We enter the double purpose office-guest room. A color TV sits on a table next to a clunky Dell computer and black-and-white ink-jet printer on a particle-board desk. Stiff hardcover books on game theory and foreign policy beckon me. Philippe's chemical engineering books, our French-English-Hebrew dictionaries, and my beloved classics like *The Clan of the Cave Bear* stand matchstick straight in the built-in shelves. He opens the storage space above the closet and tosses them in with a game-show-host *voilà*.

We switch off the light and leave.

Distort

As November rolls into
December rolls into
January, all anyone
ever talks about is
Iraq this, Kuwait that,
& war
        after Hussein attempts
        to transform what he
        initiated as an Arab-
        Arab conflict into an
        Arab-Israeli conflict,
                                but
        Israel fails to engage &
        declares a state of
                                emergency
        & puts the army on
high alert,
        delivering a karate-
        chop blow to our
        honeymoon phase
                        &
        driving my low blood
        pressure to a boil, when

@3:00 a.m. on January 18, 1991.

we hear a haunting sound, dash down
hall, grab cordless phone in kitchen,
enter guest room, turn on light, slam
door, seal with duct tape, snatch card-
board boxes from closet, rip open,
remove protective guards, don gas
masks, gag, hear husband say breathe
(try not to gag), hear rockets outside
windows covered with industrial
strength plastic sheeting, gag, hear
CNN report live in the Middle East
(try not to gag), hear phone ring, gag,
hear parents ask if we're okay as they
watch CNN report live in California
(try not to gag), hear my muffled voice
beneath hefty rubber mask say we're
okay, gag, I'm okay (try not to gag).

Hand in hand

We carry our masks everywhere: to work, to friends, to cafés. Shrill sirens ring at random times. Each one unnerves me, making me feel tiny and vulnerable. Making me curse myself, question my decisions.

One night, at the movies, we recline in frayed burgundy seats, hand in hand, laughing at small-time conman John Cusack in *The Grifters*. After the intermission (only in Israel) and before the end (just our luck), the lights go on, the actors fading out as if a director yelled, *Cut!* when we hear it: the unmistakable, high-low, up-down, ear-shrieking sound.

Ready? Philippe asks.

I ('m not, but) have no choice. I married this place as much as I married this person. We retrieve the chunky boxes underneath our chairs. We've been through this drill enough that we no longer need help fastening the masks, enough that I no longer gag, enough that I fear hearing it again.

For six weeks, Scud missiles fall, mainly hitting the greater Tel Aviv and Haifa regions. No one around us is hurt. On the surface, we're untouched. But inside, in my kishkes, everything throbs.

Tears & fears

All summer long, I cry. When little blisters form between my fingers and itch me awake at 2:00 a.m. When strangers cut in front of me in line at the grocery store. When Philippe tries to solve my tears like a calculus problem. When strangers cut in front of me in line at the post office. When Philippe doesn't try to solve my tears. When strangers cut in front of me in line at the bank. When Philippe suggests therapy. When strangers cut me off on the road. When friends suggest therapy.

Within fifteen minutes of my first session with an American psychologist (as in someone from my country and culture who speaks my language and understands my mentality) in the next neighborhood, she diagnoses me with culture shock followed by *I think your husband should join you.*

A week later, Philippe and I sit in her humdrum home-office, a standard Israeli room with speckled tiled floors and not-quite-white walls, a few framed diplomas from east coast universities on the wall above her desk.

I'm scared to start a family, I confess.

Over the past few months, he's mentioned the four-letter word beginning with the second letter of the alphabet. (Think B __ __ __.) Each time, I've conjured excuses like my thesis and my questionable career path. More confessions—about *Shabbat* and *kashrut,* about his beliefs and my doubts.

How can we raise kids if we're so different? If he doesn't accept me as I am?

Actually, he says, *she doesn't accept me as I am.*

Full-body clench: jaw, fists, shoulders.

The psychologist pauses. *So how do you want to raise your future children?*

I face my husband of two years. *If we have a boy, will he have to wear a kippah? What about girls wearing pants?*

I don't want my offspring to look different from me, to wear outward symbols of Judaism on the street, whether here or abroad. But when did I lose my voice and become so passive in our relationship?

Over the course of the next few weeks, as the country hunkers down for the holiest of days[6], we discuss a handful of kid-related hypotheticals from

---

[6] Rosh Hashanah lasts two days (considered too important to be observed for only twenty-four hours); Yom Kippur fast lasts twenty-five hours (like *Shabbat*); Sukkot lasts seven days in Israel (eight in the diaspora), the first and last days (and second and eighth days in the diaspora) are *Shabbat*-like when work is forbidden (for once, living here has an advantage)

biking and drawing on *Shabbat* to swimming and doing homework on holidays to school systems—religious vs. secular vs. pluralistic—until it feels like we're tempting fate. Until each one of my apprehensions is exposed. Until every one of my crying jags stop.

Cocoon

On September 13, 1993, we bring home our four-day-old son from the hospital. With the crib in one room and oodles of baby presents in another, our spacious apartment bursts.

Philippe urges me to rest, but I can't. All I want to do is gaze down at my infant and up at the television screen.

On CNN, Israeli Prime Minister Yitzhak Rabin and PLO leader Yasser Arafat extend arms for the first public handshake between the arch enemies, with US President Bill Clinton at their sides.

I stretch out on our autumn-colored sofa. My baby, his eyes pinched closed and his lips puckered, sleeps, oblivious to the words of import.

While Clinton speaks, I stroke the wisps of downy hair on his head, overcome by the thought that I've made this helpless, perfect being, that it's my job to protect him.

When Rabin speaks, I feel tears prick the edges of my eyes, burdened by the thought that I've settled in this sliver of land where the personal and the political are tangled, inseparable, insufferable.

As these world leaders stand on the White House lawn in Washington, D.C., thousands of onlookers applaud. For months, I've been reading, listening, paying attention to the news.

Watching these ground breakers, I wrap myself in a cocoon of illusion, believing that when my child grows up, he won't have to serve in the army. Believing there won't even be one.

Semantics

Elbow-deep in packing and preparing to move to France, we meet with our banker, who asks how long we intend to live abroad.

Shnatayim[7], Philippe says with certainty.

Lo, I insert, *camah shanim*[8].

If English has 171,146 words but Hebrew only has 33,000, how is it possible one exists to designate such a specific time frame?

Unbeknownst to my husband, I hope to prolong our one-year-MBA-in-Paris (for him), one-year-work-in-California (for me) agreement. I refuse to be encaged by nouns or numbers. Now that I'm a mother, the thought of moving, whether after two or five or seven years, seems unrealistic and overwhelming.

Philippe glowers. The banker tarries.

I huff *fine*, say *shnatayim*. Play martyr to make peace.

---

[7] *shana* = שנה = *1 year, but shnatayim* = שנתיים = 2 years... go figure!

[8] *cama shanim* = כמה שנים = some/a few years

One step outside, Philippe interrogates me like a KGB agent. *Why did you say that?*

Because who knows what can happen? Jobs, kids? Too many unknowns. We should leave it open-ended. That doesn't make sense to you?

Non, he says, walking away as the heat hammers me into the ground.

Paris

When the taxi stops in front of a brick building on a one-way street in the 3rd arrondissement, I *oh là là*. In France for Philippe's business school, we're a ten-minute walk from the Seine, Pompidou, and Place des Vosges.

Thick, wooden beams span the length of our fully-furnished, one-bedroom rental. On a scale between comfortable/10 and insufficient/1, this place is fabulous/5; our immaculate Israeli apartment with wedding presents and childhood possessions seems irrelevant.

By early autumn, our son starts daycare, I work, Philippe studies. At night in bed, we gape at the massive beams.

One Sunday, I bundle my baby in his red puffy coat and strap him in his Maclaren to meet a friend at Bois de Boulogne. Standing at the top of the stairs in Châtelet metro station, I look down. Neither an escalator nor an elevator nor any handicap-friendly access in sight. I pick up the stroller and descend. Air-raid alerts and incoming missiles traumatize me, but a European metropolis and steep stairs do not.

Green light, red light

One evening, home alone after yet another frustrating day answering phone calls from prospective students for the Council on International Educational Exchange (a.k.a. how we pay our bills), I call my brother-in-law's house in Jerusalem to speak to Philippe.

Is the baby okay? You aren't going to believe it. Everyone okay? I can't believe it. Can you talk? I need to talk. Of all the weeks for you to be away, I can't believe it's this one.

His only break from business school is now: mid-February, a week after we gave my parents the green light, telling them we were moving to Oakland after his program ended in June, giving them permission to look for a rental house.

I got the job. The one at OECD. After four rounds of interviews in the English-language publications department of Organization for Economic Cooperation and Development's sleek headquarters in the tree-lined 16th arrondissement, after months of waiting for a response, I passed.

Mazel tov! Bravo! Alors? He asks what I want to do.

When I close my eyes, geometric shapes head-on collide: ∥ vs ⊦ vs Ω Saying yes to the intergovernmental organization means a significant salary and a solid career not to mention worldwide tax exemption, but it also means changing the green light to red.

What do you think? I ask, hearing his heavy breath and the static on the other end of the line, wishing he were closer.

I'll do whatever you want. You decide.

His reaction stuns me. I snatch a tissue and wipe my eyes.

If we stay in France, I can find a job there, Philippe says. *But you'll have to tell your parents we're not coming.*

Weeping turns to sobbing as Good Jewish Daughter Guilt engulfs me.

Fight

On our last night in Paris, Philippe and I tuck our toddler into his crib then join my in-laws, here to help us pack before our imminent one-way flight to San Francisco. Earlier, while deciding what to take and what to toss, my father-in-law taught me a valuable French idiom: *Le malheur des uns fait le bonheur des autres*[9]. Thanks to a hard-core stress-induced case of laryngitis, I cannot do more than nod.

Et voilà, he says once we are seated at the table. Raising a wine glass, he focuses on his son: *Philippe, je te souhaite bonne chance à ta nouvelle vie américaine et bon courage pour trouver un boulot*[10].

Et moi? I say, straining my vocal chords. Is my face as red and as hot as it feels? After seven years of living abroad, I deserve luck too.

Unable to conceal my rage, I storm from the table. My feet stomp soundlessly on the wall-to-wall carpeting. I slam the bedroom door. Flop on the

---

[9] Leave it to the French to make the proverb *one man's trash is another man's treasure* sound beautiful

[10] I wish you good luck in your new American life and in your job hunt

bed. Hear Philippe follow. Stare at the beams. Say in my loudest, harshest whisper: *I'm invisible in your parents' eyes. Like I don't count. Like my only purpose is to bear grandchildren.*

Shhh, he strokes me, *ne t'inquiètes pas.* He could probably get a Guinness World Record for Most Overused Words.

Someone knocks, peeks in, asks to enter. The father-son physical resemblance—large heads, protruding noses, football shoulders—makes me blench. Have I overlooked their emotional one? The senior Lang doesn't have an unkind bone in his body but is so walled off when it comes to communicating. Every Friday when he calls to say *Shabbat shalom,* he hangs up after twenty-three seconds of hello, how are you, your parents, the baby? Perhaps his woodenness is because he was an only child, or because he was in hiding during the Second World War, or because he raised two boys. Or maybe it's more linguistic and cultural: reserved, polite French man versus bossy, bold American woman.

He clears his throat. *Je suis désolé si je t'ai blessé[11], Jennifer.*

Merci, I murmur, knowing he can't hear me, knowing my immature tendency to hold grudges, knowing I need to grow up.

---

[11] I'm sorry if I hurt your feelings

Root and reach

Six weeks after we settle in Oakland, a mile from my parents, I start a job in the marketing department of the San Francisco Jewish Federation and enroll in a beginner's class at Piedmont Yoga Studio. Fifty-odd men and women squeeze mat to mat.

The teacher tells us to stand tall like mountains. To press down through our feet, to anchor ourselves. He says it as if it's simple, as if feeling the earth below is possible. I jam my feet into the California wood floor, so warm and forgiving compared to Israeli tiles in our apartment.

Cool! Rodney says. *You guys look really rooted.*

We change poses. He struts around the room. His tank top reveals picture-worthy biceps. But the litany of instructions—left leg straight, right knee bent, arms parallel, tailbone down—makes my brain whizz and whir.

In Warrior pose, I relish the stretch between my ribs, down my thighs. In Pigeon pose, I enjoy the opening of my hip. But above all, I adore his language, the way he suggests where we should be in relation to terra firma. Ever since I left for college in Chicago and my junior year abroad in France over a decade earlier, nothing has felt firm.

Root down through your feet and reach up, Rodney says. His words sound like song lyrics, profound and soulful.

All I want to understand is how, after growing up in the same house-street-city-county-state-country-continent, have I ended up so rootless? Transient, unsettled, wandering, nomadic, on shaky ground.

It

Philippe and I celebrate when he receives his first offer in high-tech after a year-long job hunt. We extend the lease on our starter house and re-enroll our son in the synagogue preschool. We enjoy Rosh Hashanah and Thanksgiving meals at my parents' house. But we don't talk about *it*.

It = staying in the Bay Area, where I know short-cuts and backroads, ~~5,731 miles from France, where he knows shortcuts and backroads, 7,416 miles from Israel, where neither of us knew shortcuts and backroads~~.

We dress our son in an Elmo costume for Halloween and take a road trip to Los Angeles for a long weekend. We discuss whether or not my marketing job will make sense with two kids. We debate boys and girls names and borrow a crib, bassinet, and baby swing. But we don't talk about *it*.

It = staying in the Bay Area, where I speak in slang, acronyms, and idiomatic expressions, ~~5,731 miles from France, where he speaks in slang, acronyms, and idiomatic expressions, 7,416 miles from Israel,~~

~~where neither one of us spoke in slang, acronyms, and idiomatic expressions.~~

As our one-year-in-America agreement slides into two then three then more, elephants take cover under every rug in every room, turning the where-to-live and how-much-Judaism-to-live-by conversations taboo. We break down. Lose our bearings. Come unhinged. Wrestle, with each other, with ourselves.

Tilt

Thirty weeks thick with baby #2, I can no longer lift or lower my legs with ease, lie on my back, or bend over my body in yoga class. Upon Rodney's suggestion, I switch to the Monday night prenatal group.

In a quintessentially Californian, down-to-earth, calming voice, the teacher asks us to say our names, due dates, and any pregnancy-related woes. Seated cross-legged in a circle on the hardwood floor and surrounded by every possible prop—bolsters, blankets, blocks, chairs, straps—we each unload our end-of-the-day aggravations and bodily grievances.

A slender woman with chiseled cheek bones and honey brown hair who doesn't look pregnant from behind catches my eye. Lisa and I share the same April 18 due date, both opting for surprise, each convinced we're carrying boys.

For the next ninety minutes, we sit, stand, balance, on our own and with partners. It's not nearly as challenging as my regular practice, but it still allows me to unwind.

After class, everyone squats on the porch steps to put on shoes. The odors of onion quiche and apple tart from Chez Simone, a French café next door, drift through the evening air. Lisa and I exchange vitals like ER doctors: both Virgos, we're born one day apart, avid readers, health food freaks, and exercise addicts. A Canadian immigrant married to an American, she understands the challenges of living far from family.

So are you Jewish? she asks after I mention Israel.

I nod.

Interesting. Growing up in Winnipeg, I didn't learn a lot about Judaism.

I nod again, relieved for a friend with whom I can indulge my occasional shrimp cravings, from whom I can separate my strange pseudo-Sabbath-observant lifestyle, with whom I can simply be.

So tell me more, she says, and I tilt towards her openness.

Spoiled

For my thirty-second birthday, Philippe hands me an awkward package with a poorly-wrapped object sticking out like a telescope.

I rip off the wrapping and shriek, *C'est magnifique!* My very own yoga mat: slim, stinky, sticky, synthetic, and sapphire blue. *Best birthday present ever!* I smother him with smooches, my tongue pressing hard inside his mouth. *Je l'adore. Je t'adore.*

Gross! our preschooler says, wedging himself between our legs. Our newborn coos in her bouncy chair.

We look down, pick him up, laugh at her, and kiss.

Wh-words

After summarizing our story for the therapist, I venture into virgin territory. Since our daughter was born eighteen months ago, a wave of change has landed like a hurricane. Philippe dons a knitted kippah—all day, every day, everywhere—washes his hands and recites the prayers at our Friday dinner table. It's as if the longer we live here, the harder he holds onto religion, to keep him connected, to stay grounded. Dare I say Judaism is to him as yoga is becoming to me?

Why are you covering your head? I ask. *And what about hamotsei[12]?*

How grateful I am Dr. Plaves, an Israeli-born transplant, understands our lingo.

Our kids will learn this stuff in school, Philippe says. *We should model it. All our friends from shul do. It's no big deal.*

We joined a Modern Orthodox synagogue and enrolled our eldest in a Modern Orthodox school. (Both are really big deals.)

---

[12] הַמוֹצִיא: the blessing before breaking bread

But where's the married-couple conversation? I ask.

A freelance writer for women's websites, I read every magazine from *Parenting* to *People*. The back-page essays, often on marriage, move me. Why can't our conflicts be confined to the quotidian—duvet covers on our bed or dishes in the sink—like everybody else's?

Philippe doesn't answer. I sense a sharp lump in my throat that scalds every time I swallow.

Here and there

Outside Dr. Plaves's window, the sky is pigeon-poop grey.

I don't think I can live there, in Israel, again, I whine, sounding like a sour teenager. *Definitely not with little kids.*

Ours are five and two. Since leaving Haifa in 1994, sixteen country-wide suicide bombings have claimed 163 lives. I stroke my burgeoning belly, furious at myself for bringing another baby into our itinerant existence. Philippe slouches in his seat.

Lately, my parents and our friends have broached the forbidden question (how long are you here?), tying our tongues in knots. Unlike Princess Diana, who physically stepped onto an active minefield in Angola to aid in the call for an international ban on landmines shortly before our daughter was born, we figuratively step onto landmines when uttering words like home, roots, country.

I glare at my husband: *Do you love Israel more than me?*

No, but I don't like living here. How carelessly we combine the adverbs *here* and *there:* in this place and in that. If we're neither here nor there, are we lost? *I can't be Jewish the way I want here. You agreed to two years abroad. Remember?*

Impossible to forget. Tears snowball down my face.

The therapist observes, takes notes. I wonder what adjectives he uses to describe us, our situation: cold, complicated, unresolvable?

If I want to live in California but Philippe wants to live in Israel, then where can, where should, where will we both settle?

We leave in silence. Philippe drives. The baby kicks. I gasp.

Places left behind

One night, we lie on the living room carpet, a habit we started after our first was born and we removed our coffee table to cuddle and be closer to him on the floor.

My boss called, Philippe says, reaching for my hand. *We have to relocate, New York or Israel, or I'll lose my job.*

New York.

Everyone's predicting the local dot-com bubble's going to bust, and I don't want to be unemployed.

New York, I repeat. *Okay. As long as we buy a house.*

~~The long, miserable, depressing year it took him to find his first job in high-tech was enough for me.~~

I need to nest where I can manage mail, pay bills, and navigate healthcare in my mother tongue, where I can avoid the topic of suicide bombs altogether. In 2000, New York is relatively safe compared to Israel.

Raising kids is hard enough. I'm overwhelmed when all three need me. I can't be a good parent unless I feel secure. I don't in Israel. Do you get it?

He laces his fingers through mine.

But I can't imagine leaving my parents again. I sob. *I'm willing to move so you can keep your job, but I'm sick of feeling uprooted, never knowing how long we're staying.*

Our nonstop negotiations and mobile marriage continue. When Philippe had the jitters after our wedding a decade ago, he predicted our intractable conflict like a prophet.

No matter where we reside, one of us will always rue the loss of the place we left behind.

Twister

Okay guys and gals, this next pose isn't easy, Rodney says. (None are.) *Actually, it's really challenging.* (I have yet to strike a pose that isn't!) *It's called Garudasana or Eagle.* (What's with yoga's animal obsession?) *And it's all about balancing.* (Crap!)

It turns out that Rod, as everybody calls him, is a nationally-known yoga star who leads retreats around the world plus poster man for yoga-related accessories—mats and blocks, straps and blankets, CDs and DVDs—for Gaiam. He tells us to stand in Mountain pose, bend our knees, extend our arms to the sides, then lift our right leg and wrap it over the left as we cross the left arm under the right, bending the elbows to bring the palms together.

Oh. My. Bod.

Ground down through your feet and reach up through the crown of your head, he says.

(What the hell? Why does he always tell us to ground, to anchor, to root?)

As my body weeble-wobbles, I stifle my urge to screech.

Flow

One nothing-special Wednesday morning, a similar-age woman with ruler-straight bangs and straight hips flashes her wide American smile, introducing herself as Jennifer (ranked twentieth most popular name in 1965), explaining she's a former modern dancer turned yoga instructor (could I teach too?) with no formal training (how do you get trained?) and a Rodney replacement (five years here and never met her) even though her style is really different from his (understatement, incomparable), and for the next 120 minutes, she moves like a dervish, leading us through one long choreographed routine of ups and downs, of forwards and backwards, of rights and lefts, and as I listen to her melodious voice and mind-bending vocabulary, detecting an unfamiliar Sanskrit word starting with v[13], I am no longer in my little head, dwelling on history, revisiting crossroads, or embellishing truths, 100 percent

---

[13] Vinyasa is a style of yoga characterized by stringing postures together so that you move from one to another, seamlessly, using breath, commonly referred to as flow yoga; no two classes are ever alike

fully, totally, completely, wholly, absolutely, entirely grounded in my body, wondering if this is Rod's definition of rooted.

Predicament

Mid-winter, I board a red-eye flight to JFK solo. That Sunday, I phone Philippe from White Plains, where friends rave about its diverse Modern Orthodox community and plentiful Jewish school options, to tell him I bid on a century-old Tudor with half-moon-shaped garden, half the cost of northern California.

Are you sure? he asks.

~~I am anything but sure. I have no idea what I'm doing. I've never lived east of Illinois or bought a house. I don't love the sidewalk-less streets or snow-covered roofs but grasp our predicament.~~

The sellers accept our bid. My emotions run amuck: grateful we could afford housing (not a given in the Bay Area), relieved we're staying in America (not a given in a cross-cultural marriage), sad we're moving away from family (a given with parents in different countries), nervous we have to start anew (a given with every move). I'm empty and exhausted, and we haven't even started packing.

Of its own kind

On a quiet April evening, our children deep in dreamland, Philippe and I do what we do best: sort and sift, decide and dump.

Keep	Toss
M.A. thesis	water & electric, rental & car insurance bills
son's report cards	son's homework assignments
handmade Mother's Day & birthday cards	marketing material from work

I remember how desperate I was to leave this place after high school, I say. *Then I couldn't stand the popular crowd, the private clubs, the cliques. But now, I'm overwhelmed by its beauty.*

The San Francisco Bay Area isn't without fault, but it is sui generis. Does every young adult have to flee and grow up in order to look back with longing and appreciate their place of birth? Does everyone reach a point when they realize no place is perfect, there is no utopia?

Jennifer Lang

Philippe cradles me in his arms and listens to me blubber.

Y vs. why

After we finish arranging the basement playroom shelves with containers of Polly Pockets and Legos and Thomas the Tank Engine sets, I open the *Yellow Pages* and let my fingers walk to Y. Amid thousands of listings for everything from bakeries to nail salons, there's only one Y of interest: Yoga Haven in Tuckahoe.

Back in Alameda County, where every neighborhood has at least one studio and there's an abundance of offerings from Hatha to Bikram, Prenatal to Mommy and Me, I had choice. Here in Westchester County with its six cities, nineteen towns, and twenty-three villages, I am choice-less and lost. Last week, while looking for Mamaroneck Road in Scarsdale, I ended up on Mamaroneck Avenue and Old Mamaroneck Road in White Plains instead, pulling over and putting my head in my hands when a policeman took pity, stopped to make sure the kids and I were okay, and escorted us home. How the hell will I ever find my way to Tuckahoe?

While the kids dig for roly-polies in the backyard, I forward fold over the phone book and weep. We might still be on American soil, but it's as foreign as Mars with vinyl-sided houses, sidewalk-less streets, and no-parking-overnight rules. In Northern California, one of three people works from home as a freelancer a.k.a. consultant, but after walking around our new block and knocking on doors to introduce ourselves, I've met only doctors and bankers, accountants and attorneys. No one practices yoga.

Sticky, wet heat pierces our walls. I close the outdated weight-and-chain, wood-framed windows and turn on the bulky window air-conditioning unit. It blows air like a whale.

Ever since I first stepped on a yoga mat six years ago, the ancient practice has become my personal re-set button with its vacuum-esque powers to suction stress and negative energy in and make it vanish. Every month, when PMS attacks and turns me into a bitchy woman/bossy wife/bad mom, Philippe sends me to class. Amidst our complex checklist of needs for Jewish schools and *shuls* and commuting options for his job, I never thought about where, if at all, I'd find a yoga studio.

Why?

Why not?

Interview

One Sunday morning, as swamp-like summer humidity outside keeps us inside, we attend an Israel-related family program at *shul*. Since first stepping foot in HI (Hebrew Institute) a few weeks earlier, we've learned that the five synagogues of White Plains[14] rally together to march in the Israel Day Parade in Manhattan, raise funds for and respond to crises in the Jewish state.

After the event finishes and people mingle, a dusty blonde, bespectacled woman with a bob approaches, introducing herself as a journalist for the *White Plains Watch* newspaper, asking if she can interview me. I nod.

Why are you here? she asks.

I titter. She looks sweet like a potential friend. How to respond? Where to start? How not to dump?

Because we're new in the area and have nowhere else to go and it's really hot out and we've got nothing better to do? I half ask-half answer.

---

[14] HI & Young Israel (Modern Orthodox), Temple Israel Center (Conservative), Congregation Kol Ami (Reform), & Bet Am Shalom Synagogue (Reconstructionist) all within an easily walkable 1.8 mile radius

Nice to meet you. Welcome. I'm Cathleen, she says with a smile that makes her azure blue eyes crinkle. *Want to swap numbers?* And just like that, like Lisa, easy conversation about husbands and kids, careers and books, yoga and writing follows, inviting me to lean in.

Witness

Nine weeks after arriving in New York,
one postcard-pretty September morning,
Philippe calls from work,
his tone frantic and unfamiliar,
telling me to turn on the TV faster than fast,
so I race upstairs to my office,
where,
on my grandmother's hand-me-down black-and-white SONY set,
I bear witness to the Twin Towers blazing and smoke billowing and bodies leaping,
when a faraway voice says,

See,
    terrorism
        is
           everywhere,
                even
                    New York
                        isn't
                            safe.

No matter what

Every summer, we come to Israel to familiarize our kids with the country and their cousins, our siblings and their offspring. A non-negotiable (as long as we live in America), ~~but I don't want to be here.~~ A few years into the Second Intifada, and the number of bombings has skyrocketed.

In Jerusalem, we idle at a red light across from Machane Yehuda, a covered souk and the site of a recent suicide attack. An Egged bus sidles alongside us. I glance at Philippe: calm, focused, made of concrete. Does he see what I see? Think what I think? Can he hear my please-don't-blow-up-next-to-us thoughts?

In the backseat, our four- and six-year-old girls doze in their boosters, their nine-year-old brother in between. I scrutinize the bus of Haredi[15] boys dressed in all-black with *peyot* dangling around their ears, middle-aged men and women with empty expressions, teenaged soldiers in forest green garb with

---

[15] A very visible minority in Israel: https://www.britannica.com/topic/ultra-Orthodox-Judaism

Uzis around their necks, elderly with shopping carts and worry for them, for us, for the never-ending cycle of violence here.

Seconds before the light turns green, I shout *Go!*

Intense

Shortly after the start of our second year in White Plains, I commute fifteen minutes south to Tuckahoe five-to-six days a week. From October through March, I immerse in a 200-hour teacher-training program, thanks to Philippe's support and our life-savior au pair, spending many Sundays and evenings with twelve other yoga-obsessed women.

Together we learn about muscles and bones in *The Anatomy Coloring Book*. Read the Hindu Holy Scriptures in *The Bhagavad Gita*. Discuss ethics, meditation, and physical postures in Sri Swami Satchidananda's *The Yoga Sutras of Patanjali*. Memorize the eight limbs of yoga[16], focusing on the five yamas[17] for moral conduct and five niyamas[18] for

---

[16] Yama (abstinences), niyama (observances), asana (yoga postures), pranayama (breath control), pratyahara (withdrawal of the senses), dharana (concentration), dhyana (meditation) and samadhi (absorption)

[17] Ahimsa (non-harming or non-violence in thought, word and deed); satya (truthfulness); asteya (non-stealing); brahmacharya (celibacy or right use of energy); aparigraha (non-greed or non-hoarding)

[18] Saucha (cleanliness); santosha (contentment); tapas (discipline, austerity or burning enthusiasm); svadhyaya (study of the self and of the texts); isvara pranidhana (surrender to a higher being, or contemplation of a higher power)

healthy living and spiritual existence. (~~My new and improved and very unique Ten Commandments?~~)

In my late thirties, I am distracted from my family life, challenged by the steep learning curve, never wanting it to end, not yet grasping the emerging analogy were this an SAT question and I had to choose one answer for the following question:

Judaism : Philippe as
hunger : thirst
etiquette : discipline
love : treason
yoga : Jennifer

4 : 1

One freezing Friday night, as wind howls and trees creak and radiators clink, I tune in and out of our family chaos. In when the kids clamor for more chicken soup, out when they talk about the weekly Torah section, a core subject in their school curricula.

Who knows the Parshat HaShavuah? Philippe asks, seated at the head of the table like French monarchs: Henry IV, King Louis XIV, King Louis XVI.

Me, me, me, our youngest says, shooting her arm up like an obedient first grader. She rambles about some biblical character while I fantasize about California sun.

Bravo, Philippe praises her.

He asks age-appropriate questions to each one, a ritual he started when our son entered kindergarten. The middle one wiggles in the bentwood chair. The eldest interrupts with his older, wiser input. Before long, the four of them engage in a conversation that neither includes nor interests me.

Just like the four of them shower before *Shabbat* starts on Friday.

Just like the four of them dress up and leave for synagogue every Saturday morning.

Just like the four of them sleep outside in the sukkah every autumn.

Just like the four of them eat only kosher meat.

Our family dynamic is often 4 : 1, leaving me Odd Mom Out and uncomfortable ~~in my own home, in my own skin.~~

Truth or lie?

I climb into bed and twine my legs around Philippe. Between the flannel sheets and his body heat, I warm up quickly.

I want to sign up for a yoga workshop next weekend at Sage. Awash in sunlight, the studio is a solid twenty-minute freeway ride north in Armonk, the opposite direction from Tuckahoe. Its semolina yellow walls bounce off the hardwood floors, casting light even on dark winter days. *I'll be back for dinner on Friday and leave after you go to shul on Saturday.*

I prefer you not drive, he says. I unwrap my legs. *For the kids.*

Sometimes he speaks in code, in half-truths, even un-truths; surely he's more concerned about someone from our community seeing me than our children.

Sometimes I speak in code, in half-truths, even un-truths; rarely do I discuss my Jewish husband or holidays with my yoga-teacher world.

Are you kidding me? My body temperature plummets.

He suggests I sleep at the studio owner Susan's place on Friday, return Saturday night.

Jennifer Lang

Like I can't come and go as I please?
No response.
Like my absence is better—for the kids?
Tension is so loud it rumbles in my ears. In the dimness, I think about how far I've derailed from my dreams, how long ago I lost my inner compass, and how desperate I am to find my way back.

Corpse

At the end of a ninety-minute kick-ass yoga class at Sage, I succumb. Lying flat on our backs for the final resting pose, Susan guides us into Savasana. The room hushes. Nobody stirs. My mind blurs. Back in California, the mere mention of the pose triggered a Pavlovian reaction to roll up my mat and tiptoe out the door. (Why pay a babysitter or miss work time to lie down and close my eyes? We never did that in my modern dance class.) For years, Rodney and Jennifer the Dancer and the prenatal teacher tried convincing me to stay, insisting it was the most important posture. Then, I didn't understand that the point of the practice wasn't to perfect handstand or balance in crow but to help the body transition from flight-or-fight mode, to access the parasympathetic nervous system, to restore, renew, replenish.

Then, I couldn't figure out why everybody else considered it their favorite pose.

Now I do.

Surprise

That August, we land in Israel a week after a United Nations-brokered ceasefire, putting an end to a thirty-four-day military operation with Lebanon, to celebrate our son becoming a bar mitzvah.

One night, Philippe and I check into a hotel, leaving the kids with my parents. I lie belly-down on the king-size bed, watching him shave, admiring how trim and muscular he is at forty-one.

Did I tell you my boss wants to retire next year? He asked if I'm interested in replacing him, managing the Israel office.

Wow. I feign excitement. *What did you say?*

That it probably won't happen. That you'd never want to come.

I pause. *This might surprise you.* Another pause. *But what if I said I'm open to the idea of living here—for a year?* He turns off his electric razor. *I've been thinking a lot about raising children here.* Ours thrive on walking with their cousins to the park and pizzeria, such unfamiliar freedoms for American schoolchildren. *I'm pretty set professionally.* He listens. *I can write and teach yoga anywhere.*

Now that the kids are more independent, that get-up-and-go part of me has begun to resurface. Israel isn't my dream destination, but it is the easiest. Fear and safety are no longer my ammunition since suicide bombings have dramatically dwindled with the newly-built ~~albeit controversial~~ separation wall.

So let's keep talking about it, he says. *We'll keep it open?* He kisses my head.

Family tree

Showered and dressed in our bar mitzvah bests, we gather on the grass outside Kibbutz Gal On guesthouse bungalows with our invitees. The photographer places the five of us between two acacia trees. Slowly, our groupings grow: Philippe's side of the family, my side, both sides, a forty-something, four-generation clan. Our teenager gapes.

This is just family? he says. *I can't believe how many of us there are. Here!*

2.1.3

Days go unmarked—Groundhog, Valentine's, Presidents'—until one exceptionally subzero Wednesday when Philippe works from home, and we decide it's time. As the kids file in the side door after school, we surprise them.

Family meeting, I say.

They remove backpacks, coats, and shoes.

In the living room, Philippe adds.

They enter wide-eyed and squish together on the two-seater sofa.

We've got big news, I say, *and no, it's not a baby.*

They've asked.

We're going away next year. Guess where, Philippe adds.

Number 2 speaks first: *France?*

We shake heads.

Number 1 comes next: *Israel?*

We nod.

No, tell me you're kidding? he says, his still-little-boy voice aquiver. *I'm gonna miss my freshman year of high school here?* As his eyes well, Philippe bear-hugs him.

Number 3 screams: *I don't want to go to Israel! I don't want to leave my best friend! I don't want to miss third grade!*

I scoop her into my arms, reciting unrehearsed platitudes like *I know a year seems long* and *change can be scary, but it'll go by quickly* and *we'll come back* to reassure 3, 2, 1, me, trying not to cry.

On some stranger's bed

As soon as I walk in the door and plop my purse on the living room ledge, the keys clang against the cold, common Israeli tile, making me shudder.

You have plans? Philippe asks. It's 8:00 a.m., and I've already dropped off the kids at Hebrew *ulpan* in the center of Raanana, a residential city northeast of Tel Aviv and his company's headquarters. The oppressive end-of-August heat sucks my energy.

Nothing special, I say with acerbity. *Meeting a complete stranger for coffee.*

I've agreed to meet an American immigrant, who has no clue it's my forty-second birthday. Under normal circumstances, I would have welcomed the diversion except now nothing is normal or familiar.

I remove my sandals. Climb the stairs to the bedroom, the gelid floor cooling the soles of my swollen feet. Curl up in a fetal position on the bed.

(Why did I agree to spend a year in a country that feels so familiar yet brings out the worst in me?)

When we first discussed the Year of Living Differently to submerge the kids in Israeli culture,

I was excited. As middle age dawned, the school-work-vacation routine was becoming predictable. A younger, buried version of me woke up, yearned for adventure. Workwise, it was easy for both of us. Yet, now, I long for everything I left behind: English-language radio stations, friendly drivers, well-mannered grocery/postal/bank clerks.

After a long cry, I stare in the mirror. A grown, confident woman with a fierce gaze stares back. Enough! I'm determined to reconcile my divided selves: the me that craves newness and the me that needs structure and control, even if they might forever remain at odds.

Heavy

Midway through our year, Philippe and I meet in Manhattan, each of us there for work. Crushed by jet lag, we collapse into bed. In the obscurity, I initiate an eggshell-fragile conversation. *It took being back here to realize I don't want to stay in Israel. I miss my professional life. Polite people. Easy communication. Customer service. Here's home.*

You're being unfair.

No, you're being unfair. We agreed to one year. Why are you going back on your word? Like you're betraying me.

You did it first!

Who sounds more childish—him or me? Regardless, his words bite, but I remember when I refused to return to Israel a decade prior. Now I understand what it feels like when your spouse has deceived or abandoned you, backpedaling on your plans, discounting your feelings. Cactus-prickly silence nestles between us in the queen-size bed. The city surges with sound: ambulance sirens scream, taxi drivers rumble, a lone musician strums a guitar.

I gaze at the ceiling, picturing the wooden beams in our Parisian apartment, awed by their durability. If only marriage could be as resilient.

Why aren't you at least open to staying? he asks. *I can see you question it sometimes.*

Shortly after we settled six months ago, he and our son declared their desire to stay in Israel permanently. Philippe bikes to work and rejoices on the holidays, whether religious or secular, each marked with a ceremony, a fast, a parade. Our typical Israeli teenager bikes/buses/walks everywhere, so comfortable in his country of birth. Not me. Between the girls' six-day school week and midday dismissal, our abbreviated one-day weekend ~~when Philippe won't drive, spend money, or use electricity~~, and the sheer smallness of the country, I feel suffocated.

The next day, while packing, we fold our anger into the creases of our shirts and tuck it into the hems of our pants, making our suitcases overweight.

Back in White Plains,

we sprint to couples' counseling.
During our first session, Philippe
and I recap our year abroad: the
highs, the lows, the breaking points
between. Like Dr. Plaves, Dr.
Jackie assigns homework: spend
together time alone weekly, compli-
ment each other daily, and share
three things we appreciate about
each other nightly. In the beginning, we see her regularly, then
less regularly, then rarely, eventu-
ally agreeing to return as needed.
Slowly, as the northeast winter
wanes, the arctic wall of ire begins
to thaw. In the dawning of spring,

hope blooms.

Schedule

One Tuesday morning, a new student enters the door at Sage and asks if I'm gentle Jen. My entire upper body convulses with a loud, genetic cackle. *If you were to ask anyone in my family, they'd say no, but sure, you can call me that.*

Like salsa, I like taking and teaching spicy flow practices. But I lost my time slot at the studio when we spent that year in Israel, and the only way to get back on the schedule was to start a gentle class.

My new students are either older, out of shape, exercise avoiders, or injured. As the weeks pass and the group grows, I listen to their stories of chronic pain or arthritic wear and tear or scoliosis or auto-immune diseases. I smile when they ask if it's Savasana time yet. I observe their bodies, what they can and cannot do, see their faces wince when they've reached their limit.

As the seasons change, I step deeper and deeper into their shoes, feeling compassion drown me, embodying gentle Jen.

Sigh. Silence. Dread.

The following autumn, after the kids enter middle and high school, our eleventh grader joins us on the living room sofa. When I mention the upcoming college fair, he says he isn't going.

Sigh.

When I ask why, he says he's enlisting in the Israel Defense Forces after graduation.

Silence.

Like every Israel-born Jew, our son is obligated to serve at eighteen. But because we moved abroad when he was a baby, he could opt out.

Philippe utters words that are un-utterable for me: *If that's what you want to do, we'll support you.*

Dread.

We left that distant land for Philippe, but we've stayed away for—because of—me. While I cannot deny my son his dream, I also cannot imagine shipping him off alone to a country where soldiers are often criticized by the greater world but pampered by their parents.

His decision to serve means Philippe and I have to go around every room and lift every rug and drag out every elephant. It also means that after a decade and a half in my homeland, my time here is coming to an end.

Slay

During our long overdue Dr. Jackie session, I unload my pent-up emotions from resentment to contentment. For me and my girls. About Israel and its army. About our safety and our psyches. Our son wants to enlist, but if we go, the girls will be drafted.

She asks if there's anything good about going. I tell her no more private Jewish school tuition, basement floods, or snow days. She eyes Philippe.

I'm only here because of her, he says. *I feel dead in America.*

Gulp. (Am I guilty of sentencing my husband to death in American suburbia, or is it living in the diaspora that has slayed his spirit? Who have I put first: myself or our children?)

Philippe turns toward me. *I know you don't want to leave. I know it's hard for you. But will you think about this seriously?*

I wipe my eyes and wonder about our family divide, about the Women of the Book. If we go, will Philippe and I swap places: he'll come alive, while *I'll* wither? For I am more ruthless than Ruth-ish, unable to embrace her words to her mother-in-law: Whither thou goest, I will go; thy people shall be my people, thy God, my God.

Calculation

6 years in Israel

+

14 years in America

=

Surrender

Like a losing candidate in a skewed election, I concede.

Sacred

At our Thursday afternoon teachers' practice, Susan starts with Anusara[19] yoga talk. One day, she regales us with battle stories between Krishna and Arjuna from *The Bhagavad Gita,* another, she dives deep into the concept of grace. Today is about rooting down to find stability, then reaching up toward freedom. Like Rodney on steroids: better, louder, clearer.

After balancing on our hands in crow pose, she cues us to slowly put our heads onto the floor, pull into our center, and extend our legs up into headstand. *Don't be scared of falling out of the pose,* she says. I contract my abdomen and focus. *Move slowly. You can go to the wall or put a blanket near your hands, whatever makes you feel safe. But remember, it's okay to fall.*

I'm not a faller. Whether skiing, biking, or hiking, I'll stay on the path, slow down, or bow out altogether rather than dare and go beyond my comfort

---

[19] Founded by American yoga teacher John Friend in 1997, this school of yoga is grounded in a Tantric philosophy of intrinsic goodness, Anusara means flowing with Grace, flowing with Nature and following your heart, as interpreted from the Sanskrit anusāra, meaning "custom, usage, natural state or condition"

zone. Falling terrifies me. In fifth grade, after landing wrong on my wrist while doing a backbend to show off for my grandma and spending all summer in a cast at camp, I stay low to the ground: safe.

Think about it, Susan says. Her walnut colored ponytail swipes side to side like windshield wipers. *If you don't occasionally fall and you always stay comfortable with the poses you won't grow. Your poses won't change.*

I glance at the group—Wendy with her vibrant rose vine tattoos on her forearms, Christine with her deep-set opaque eyes, Robin with her tight ringlets, and Lisa with her cheerleader smile—and sigh. For two hours every week we gather to practice the physical poses and gab about the business of teaching, about our students' issues, about injury-related questions, but rarely do we stop moving, face each other, and open up about our personal lives. They know nothing of my mixed marriage and our country-religion conundrum. They have no clue that I turn into Cinderella every Friday afternoon as darkness descends and *Shabbat* begins.

As I weigh *Watchasana,* a Susan expression to sit and observe other yogis practice, I touch down. Place my crown on my mat. Suck in my belly. Push up my legs. Flex, then point, then floint—another Susanism for flex-point the feet to engage the muscles in the legs.

I'm up. I'm straight. I'm strong. I'm free.

Krishna Das, an American vocalist who sings Hindu devotional music called kirtans, croons on the playlist: *Om Namah Shivaaya,* the Sanskrit slipping in and out of my ears like prayer, words about bowing to Shiva, to my own true self, to teachers who took care of me when I couldn't take care of myself. To Rodney. To Jennifer. To Susan.

Off balance

Less than twenty-four
hours after revealing the
we're-moving-to-Israel-again
news to our kids, I renege.
*I know we agreed to come
back next year.*
Philippe eyes me with
distrust.
But I can't.

I loathe our one-sided
conversations, his silence,
my voice.
*It's just so lopsided. All about
you. For you. Because of you.*
I think of the word
imbroglio and how
each of its three defini-
tions apply: a misunder-
standing, disagreement
of a complicated or
bitter nature, as between
persons or nations; an
intricate and perplexing
state of affairs, a complicated or tough situation;
and a confused heap.
The issue is no longer
how we've gotten into
this mess, but if we'll ever
get out.

Conjugation

Early September, two days after our twentieth wedding anniversary, Philippe and I sit on the brown suede sofa in our New York Tudor sunroom, sleep-deprived, sad, pensive. Heat makes the fabric stick to the backs of my thighs. The kids (thank you-know-who) are out at playdates.

Who or what do you love more: Israel or me? I ask—not the first time.

I love you. I want to be with you. He reaches for my hands. *But I can't stay here.*

I swallow. Stop breathing. Squirm.

But you said...

To say:

Present
I say
he says

Preterite
I said
he said

Present perfect
I have said
he has said

Present perfect continuous
I have been saying
he has been saying

Throughout the month-long high holidays—a constant reminder of how much they control our lives and how hard we work to mark them—I picture the five of us floating in different parts of the planet. The only way to keep everyone together is to move to the Middle East, but I refrain from *saying* it aloud.

Coordinates

41.0340° N, 73.7629° W

vs.

32.1848° N, 34.8713° E

Towards. back. in

Still September, we tell Dr. Jackie we want to stay together.

She leans toward us.

I can give you the flashlight.

She leans back.

But I can't walk you out of the tunnel.

She leans in again.

You're going to have to figure that out together.

Tunnel thoughts close in on me.

What if we never reach the other end?

me!

In October, we face each other in a triangle. Dr. Jackie waits. Philippe starts.

I'm sorry I ever asked her to keep Shabbat, to do things that made her so uncomfortable.

I sigh. Snivel. Shake. Whisper *thank you*. Sense that phantom weight that's been squatting on my shoulders for the past two decades melt. Ponder that younger version of me: the one who didn't know how to say no in a new relationship, how to preserve her identity.

But if I can forgive him, then shouldn't I also forgive her?

me at 23?

me at 31?

me at 37?

me at 28?

me at 40?

me at 34?

me at 45?

me?

Stay, go?

Between Halloween and Thanksgiving, we stuff dressy clothes into our Honda Odyssey minivan and drive to a Philadelphia suburb for a family bar mitzvah. Between Friday night dinner and dessert, my cousin summons me.

Take a seat, Marty says, patting an empty chair. *Which way are you leaning—stay or go?*

He tilts his head toward mine. We're four years apart and close. His oversized ears make me smile.

I'm so torn. Utterly distraught.

Okay. Your son's going to the army, right?

Nod.

And you love your husband, right?

Nod again.

And he loves you?

Another nod.

A child of divorced parents, Marty has always played the peacemaker role.

You know what this means, right? I stare at him: more a sibling to me than my own. *You have to go. You have to support him even if he says he doesn't want you there. You have to keep your family together.*

A three-second shiver runs through me. Like my body understands what my brain fights.

Go

In synagogue, I chat with my camp friend Andrea, who lives nearby and who wants to know our Israel verdict.

I cross and uncross my legs. Take a deep breath. Summarize the intense conversations. Regurgitate the emotional therapy sessions.

You two have always figured it out—here and there. You wouldn't still be married if you hadn't. You should go.

In that moment, I remember us as lighthearted young women in Israel, when she suggested I write a pro-con list about living with Philippe. My eyes mist.

It's like you know something I don't or believe in me, in us when I can't, I say. *Thank you.*

After the bar mitzvah luncheon, my girls jump like jellybeans. *Can we go to the hotel to swim with our cousins, please?* they plead, pressing palms together.

Without consulting Philippe, I agree. They clap and squeal, as if given permission to buy anything they want at the mall.

You'll tell Abba? the thirteen-year-old asks.

Hopeful that their father will neither judge his daughters nor criticize me for allowing them to ride in a car with their cousins on *Shabbat,* I blow her a kiss. While they walk away, I wonder if this is what Dr. Jackie meant about the flashlight. If I've been holding it the whole time.

Days after we return from our road trip, I beckon Philippe to the living room carpet. We sprawl, spread eagle. Our house has exquisite crown moldings but no wooden beams.

I roll onto my side. He faces me. We gawp at each other's eyes. His are 88% dark chocolate and delicious. I recap everything that transpired in Philadelphia. He listens.

Change is possible. I can change. You can change. We can move to Israel, adapt to the changes. I'll go. I agree. But there's one more thing.

Deep breath.

I need to be myself. To do Judaism my way—not yours. The kids have learned the laws of the Sabbath and kashrut and will be old enough to decide how and if they want to observe.

Finally, I've found my compass.

He inches his body toward mine, closing the space between us, and strokes my side, my waist, my hip.

Je t'aime.

Moi aussi, je t'aime.

Self-talk

I count time in terms of losses and lasts: stunning fall foliage, dreaded snow days, sacred yoga teachers' practice. And then I muster mantra-ish self-talk. To remind myself that change can be difficult. That it means loss. But that we are fortunate. We have choices. Change can also bring good. The good part is up to me. To us.

Frame

On Tuesday, August 23, 2011, our driver honks three hours before our one-way flight from Newark to Tel Aviv. We do one final walk through the house. Where our children hosted countless sleepovers and birthday parties. Where they rescued a trapped possum they named Puma. Where they biked, rollerbladed, and skateboarded down the long driveway. Where they built snowmen and made forts. Where we played hide-and-seek.

Do we have everything? Philippe asks.

I clutch the ledge of the cranberry pink kitchen tiles.

The contents of our home are elsewhere, packed and sent six weeks earlier. All that remains is a frame.

Philippe encircles me in his hunky arms. Leads me out the door. Locks it behind us. Our kids wave us into the car. As the driver turns left onto Soundview, I look back, glimpse the expansive, tree-lined street, and inhale deep into my belly.

It's impossible in that moment to know what lies ahead.

All I know now is that I must turn on the flashlight and follow it. In the car, I face forward and exhale. Ready. Here we come.

Acknowledgements

So much gratitude to so many people.

Thank you Sharon Epel for bringing me on board at BabyCenter in San Francisco and editor-in-chief Clare Ellis for encouraging me to jump off the diving board and write my raw, real truth. If it weren't for you two cheering me on, I probably wouldn't be a writer.

Rebecca McClanahan, thank you for reciting a poem at the beginning of every class at Hudson Valley Writers Center in Sleepy Hollow, New York. Every time I teach, I still hear your sweet, southern voice in my ears.

Thank you to all of my workshop leaders and mentors at Vermont College of Fine Arts, but especially Sue William Silverman and Bob Vivian for planting the seed that the story of my moves should be a book, Patrick Madden for suggesting I write about my marriage, and Barbara Hurd for inspiring me to play on the page whether with words or form. And to my greater VCFA community, some of whom I've met in real life and others only on the page, I appreciate your honest feedback and unconditional support and constant pushes to dig deeper so, so much: Les W., Megan Vered, Ryder Sollmann Wyatt, Amy Mindell, Stephanie Barton, Anne McGrath, Megan Baxter, Allison Hart, Jenny Thornburg, Whitney Lee You, Emily Weinstein, Weyshawn Koons, Julie Hall Cole, Linda Murphy Marshall, Jeannine Ouellette, Mary Brindley, Kelly Beard, Kristie Frederick Daugherty, Andrea Gilham Simpson, Camilla Sanderson, Cheryl Crabb, Allison Hong Merrill, and many more. Nina Gaby, Alice Lowe, and Magin LaSov Gregg, tremendous gratitude for reading, re-reading, and re-re-reading.

Thank you Piedmont Yoga Studio founder Rodney Yee for your powerful, on point word choice. On the opposite coast, thank you Betsy Kase for certifying me and Susan Rubin for showing me that there's always room for more.

Thank you Dr. Plaves and Dr. Jackie for helping us see the cracks and rebuild our foundation.

Amie McCracken and Jessica Bell, Vine Leaves Press Publishers Extraordinaire, I loved you from your tag line: *We are a nomad publisher. Our feet are spread all over the globe.* Thank you for inviting me into your beautiful family of readers and writers.

As for the hard facts, thank you to the scientists and engineers behind ARPANET, paving the way for the INTERNET as we know it. Seriously grateful for the following sites:

Google Translate for English to French, English to Hebrew

Chabad.org for the 39 prohibited activities ("Seesaw")

Google Maps for distances in miles ("Stuck", "It")

YouTube for "Signing of the Israeli-Palestinian Declaration of Principles 1993" on Clintonlibrary42 ("Cocoon")

Ekhartyoga.com for yamas and niyamas ("Intense")

Theconjugator.com for to say ("Conjugation")

Latlong.net ("Coordinates")

Yogapedia.com for Anusara page ("Sacred")

The following vignettes were previously published:

Baltimore Review: "Naïve," "Jitters," "Here and there," and "Places left behind" were excerpted from "Uprooted," First Place contest winner, 2019

Crab Orchard Review: "Cocoon," "Family Tree," "2, 1, 3," and "Sigh. Silence. Dread." were excerpted from "The Fabric of Peace," Finalist in John Guyon Literary Nonfiction Prize, 2018

Hippocampus Magazine: "How?" was excerpted from "Gas Masks and Wedding Vows," 2016

Foreign language and transliteration

Hebrew uses the Hebrew alphabet. In this book, I wrote some words in Hebrew and transliterated certain words and expressions in the Roman alphabet. When it comes to transliteration, there are many ways to spell some words.

Places We Left Behind
Reader's Guide

1. In "Seesaw," Philippe asks Jennifer: *"Do you think you could do Shabbat more like me?"* Do you think one person has the right to ask another to change like that? Do you think he crosses a relationship boundary? Do you think she did the right thing, agreeing to accommodate him? Or is she making a bigger deal out of it than she should?

2. In "Sides," Jennifer writes a pro-con list about staying in Israel. Do you think she should have left the country since the cons outweighed the pros?

3. In "Green light, red light," Jennifer mentions Good Jewish Daughter Guilt for the first time. What does she mean? Regardless of your religion, do you relate? Why or why not? In what ways?

4. In "Fight," Jennifer storms out of a family dinner with her in-laws. Is she being overly dramatic? Childish? When have you found yourself being overly emotional, and why?

5. What happens in the chapter "Places left behind"? Are they asking too much of each other? How much can one person compromise in a relationship without being resentful?

6. In "Of its own kind," Jennifer reflects on home. Do you agree with her statement: "Does every young adult have to flee and grow up in order to look back with longing and appreciate their place of birth? Does everyone reach a point when they realize no place is perfect, there is no utopia?"

7. In "Slay," the narrator writes "For I am more ruthless than Ruth-ish, unable to embrace her words to her mother-in-law: Whither thou goest, I will go." Do you think one person in a marriage should follow/move/go where the other goes regardless?

8. What do you think is the defining moment, the turning point when Jennifer lets go of all that she is holding onto, all the obstacles in her way, and knows she will stay in the marriage and keep the family together and move?

9. There are times when Jennifer and Philippe's marital tug of war seems insurmountable. Why do you think they stayed together?

10. Physical attraction aka sex aka chemistry plays a big role in their relationship. Do you think that's important or a set-up for failure?

11. Towards the end, in "Go," Jennifer gives her daughters permission to drive in a car on *Shabbat* and swim with their cousins without consulting Philippe. Do you think that she had the right to make that decision if they had agreed to raise their kids as Sabbath observant Jews? Is that giving mixed messages? Do you think the girls asked because even though they were being raised as observant they sensed the differing viewpoints and practices of their parents?

12. In "Self-talk," Jennifer reflects on change: "To remind myself that change can be difficult. That it means loss. But that we are fortunate. We have choices. Change can also bring good." What do you feel or think about change? How do you respond to it?

13. Jennifer pushes boundaries and plays with form. At what point do you start to notice what she's doing with the prose? Does it enhance or interfere with the story? What does the box represent in "Back in White Plains"? What do you think is the difference between her use of strikethroughs vs parentheses? Why do you think she chose to relay certain information as endnotes rather than within the text?